PRAISE FOR *LATE TO THE SEARCH PARTY*

"*Late to the Search Party* reads like the kind of collection a poet builds toward their entire career—that it's Steven Espada Dawson's debut is frankly a little absurd. The poems are formally brilliant, twisting received forms and inventing new ones to reflect the unprecedented irreplaceable lives that animate them. But it's the poems' psychospiritual maturity that feels really dazzling—Dawson rebukes lazy cynicism and defensive self-exonerating, again and again choosing rigor and complication over easy bromides. These are poems by a poet who has clearly done the work in the library stacks and in their own heart."

—Kaveh Akbar, author of *Martyr!*

"How do you carry your family with you when you're the only one who has survived the furies of life? That impossible question drives this debut poetry collection. In these exquisitely crafted elegies, Steven Espada Dawson writes of how addiction and absence and illness and grief can become a new center of gravity. The poems in *Late to the Search Party* stitch together the memories of a family torn apart by circumstance, with threads of beauty, joy, rage, and undying love."

—Roxane Gay, author of *Bad Feminist*

"*Late to the Search Party* is an astonishing first book. Steven Espada Dawson's elegies are searing, brilliantly built, gorgeous, and heartrending. Vulnerability and craft are inseparable. I felt many things while reading these poems. Sorrow. Admiration. Wonder. Dawson is a magnificent poet and I am thankful for these poems."

—Eduardo C. Corral, author of *Guillotine*

T0349401

LATE TO THE SEARCH PARTY

POEMS

STEVEN ESPADA DAWSON

SCRIBNER

NEW YORK   AMSTERDAM/ANTWERP   LONDON
TORONTO   SYDNEY/MELBOURNE   NEW DELHI

Scribner

An Imprint of Simon & Schuster, LLC

1230 Avenue of the Americas

New York, NY 10020

This book is a work of fiction. Any references to historical events, real people,
or real places are used fictitiously. Other names, characters, places,
and events are products of the author's imagination, and any resemblance to
actual events or places or persons, living or dead, is entirely coincidental.

First Scribner trade paperback edition May 2025

SCRIBNER and design are trademarks of Simon & Schuster, LLC

Simon & Schuster strongly believes in freedom of expression and stands against
censorship in all its forms. For more information, visit BooksBelong.com.

For information about special discounts for bulk purchases, please contact
Simon & Schuster Special Sales at 1-866-506-1949 or business@simonandschuster.com.

The Simon & Schuster Speakers Bureau can bring authors to your live event.
For more information or to book an event, contact the Simon & Schuster Speakers Bureau
at 1-866-248-3049 or visit our website at www.simonspeakers.com.

Interior design by Kyle Kabel

Manufactured in the United States of America

1 3 5 7 9 10 8 6 4 2

Library of Congress Cataloging-in-Publication Data is available.

ISBN 978-1-6680-8156-3
ISBN 978-1-6680-8158-7 (ebook)

for my mother, first, and then for my brother

A hole is nothing
but what remains around it.

—Matt Rasmussen, *Black Aperture*

He told me I shouldn't smile, that this whole party was shit
because I'd imagined it all.

—Natalie Diaz, *When My Brother Was an Aztec*

CONTENTS

LATE TO THE SEARCH PARTY

A RIVER IS A BODY RUNNING

The first time I found my brother
overdosed, he looked holy. A thing
not to be touched. Yellow halo of last
night's dinner. His skin, blanched blue
fresco: Patron Saint of Smack. A cop,
flustered, tugged up his shorts, plunged
a needle into a pale thigh. He hissed
awake like a soda can. The paramedic
spoke softly in his ear like a lover,
asked him what color yellow and red
make. What is the difference between
a lake and a river? In the corner
I whittle that used syringe into
an instrument only I can play.

I

WHEN THE BODY SAYS NO BUT
YOU CAN'T STOP SWALLOWING

after "On Being Suicidal" by b: william bearhart

From twenty yards away the adult megaplexxx sign
looks like a crescent moon stuck on its beetle back.

On the bus I use my fingernail to etch figure eights
into a Styrofoam cup. The mean idea of vanishing

myself is a seed I can't unplant. A stranger tells me
her kidney stones ache. Every flaw in the road

rattles her like a handful of glass. I pine for
that gorgeous myth of childhood. How I lost

good sleep worrying over watermelon seeds.
Thought they'd gut sprout, impale upward, straight

through God's windshield. The thought of being
dead returns unwelcome as a landlord.

In Colorado I pushed two motel beds together,
left the door wide open. Anything to be held

while unrecognizable. Regarding wellness
checks: I cut into a forearm length of bread,

finessed the knife like a violin bow. I tried
to convince that angry cop I never swallowed,

then threw up in his back seat. Had instead
he been my father opening, for me, a door—

not out but toward somewhere tender. Had he
held me there, so I might practice delight.

ELEGY FOR BRIAN, MY BROTHER WHO
HAS BEEN MISSING FOR TEN YEARS

At the laundromat off Guadalupe I find
out you are dead, my ear wet-ringed
to the cell phone. My load of darks spinning
in the dryer's black hole Hula-Hoop.

When I find out you have died, I am playing
miniature golf with Jules. The only course
in Georgetown, Colorado. I cheat
that last hole in one, chuck the ball

through that clown's front teeth. I am reading
peacefully, Voigt's *Headwaters*, in bed
when I get the call. At Shapiro's Deli
I eat the best Reuben of my life

and you die mid-bite. I taste it. I won't eat
sauerkraut anymore. I am at the bus stop.
I can't tell if that man is whacking weeds
or metal-detecting. You didn't die then,

but I was waiting for you to. The truth is, I'm
always waiting. Is that a field of dandelions
he is headed toward? No, they're yellow
flags meant for marking gas lines.

HOMESICK SONNET

Three blocks east a wrecking ball wears the dust
of your old house. Red wallpaper like blush across its cheeks.
The Library Tower is a broomstick Mom pretends
to bang on God's floorboards. He went for tortas
and left the stereo on. Three blocks west a woman you know
is shot while eating breakfast. The rattled cop missed his mark,
feels himself unlucky. The chilaquiles still softening
in her gut. In Boyle Heights you're still young. You fill found
condoms with hose water your neighbor calls *city punch*.
Those ribbed bladders made from Magnums, too tough
for water fights. Every balloon is a gun. A gunshot, unmistakably
loud. Your brother jokes—what kinds of apples grow on trees?
All *of 'em, stupid*. What sounds follow you away
from home? All of them. You left. All of them.

FROM THE WINDOW, MY GOWNED MOTHER
SALVAGES THE LANDSCAPE

and convinces herself the smog sunset is natural.
You can only see this purple here, she says,
that four-knuckled sky, the same purple as bruises.

My brother can barely keep himself up
-right waiting for visiting hours. His head

dipping slowly, a top failing its final turn. Coming down
from that last thick heroin hit. Sunday's surgeon
took eight bulbs from behind

Mom's left breast. Bulbs, she says, as if maybe
a source of light or crocuses flowering.

Anything to avoid the cliff-hanger t of malignant.

Brother, you wear long sleeves to hide the pinholes
freckling your arm. From three floors down
you feel her vein's blowout bloom through the fabric.

She's wrong, brother. You can see this purple everywhere.

EVERY WORD IS MY MOTHER'S

favorite fruit. A billion moths
skulk toward their final

curtain. Outside my window
each flash of blue

is a small death too, that proud bug
zapper swung above a neighbor's porch.

Mom says she's scared of ladders,
not heights, something about her spine

pressed up against the world.
While standing outside her hospital door

a crowd of doctors promised me
there is no such thing as dying

of old age. Every body fails
from something more precise—

a heart's clumsy rhythm, a tumor's slick
migration. I want so badly to write words

with a future attached. I'd kiss each one
good night, tuck them deep inside

my friends' dimples. I haven't forgotten
there is so much that is perfect.

A lover's well-perched hand, Saturn's
galactic pizza cutter. Every smile now

is an accident I want to apologize for.
Over the phone, I hear her, my mother,

plucking rubies from a pomegranate.
In Spanish, they're called granadas,

from *grenade*. When I ask why,
she tells me they explode.

ORCHARD

the first oncologist   of many
    pinched his fingers together
as if to say microscopic

the tumors first   wander
-lust the field
from breast to ovaries   finally

brain   he uses fruit now
to explain their swell
    fruit is easy to picture
ripening

in two weeks a cherry pit
becomes a cherry in eight
years an apple seed   becomes

an orchard   your body   unable
    to harvest itself

eventually the kernel
budding   behind your

right eye is a grape
-fruit quivering
    on its stem

WHEN MY BROTHER VISITS WE PLAY HIDE-AND-SEEK

with Santiago's VCR. The black ribbon of *Como agua*
para chocolate still treadmilling inside. If the new kid

is working the pawnshop, we'll have enough to split
Pioneer Chicken, fryer grease baptizing our knuckles.

Next week we'll lift a fistful of Tío's dirt weed—his rocking
chair cure for foggy eyes. Then, Mom's grocery bag

stash of laundromat quarters. Gravity stretched it thin
enough to see the tidy stacks of guillotined fathers.

Us, less scared of La Jura, more scared of her—
only one we knew could square up and make even

God flinch. My brother and me practiced hiding
so much, we eventually lost each other.

Him paddling down any river that'd end
at the tributary below a tourniquet. I learned

you can lose yourself in someone else's losing.
It took a dozen years of feeling

around in the dark for me to find a family
photo with everyone in frame. When I saw it

my eyes fogged too. In my periphery
I saw my mom, firing pearls from a slingshot.

She's got a target in mind but won't say
who. One by one I see them pass through

the sky like a needle through denim.
I'm still waiting for them to land.

ON INHERITANCE

In ninth grade I shattered
Mom's gloved hand with the first curve
-ball I threw correctly. She took Vicodin
and smiled. Her swollen fingers
looked like dates on a vine. She gave me half
a thumbs-up. We stopped playing
catch. Stopped role-playing
sitcom families.
I shaved my patchy
mustache with a disposable Venus
razor I found in her shower.
A dozen flecks pushed up
through new skin, pooling.
I dabbed that blood with
toilet paper, then couldn't
recognize half my face.

ON SAFETY

when the firefighters found my brother
in the overturned knot
                     of a volkswagen beetle
they were surprised to see
an unmangled body.
                       pristine if not for his head,
basketball swollen and blushing.

he lay calmly across the back seat, as if waking from a nap
      or ready to be drawn, there, against the aluminum
rib cage of two ruined cars. they said being a junkie
saved his life. had instead he been sober
and upright, alert—had he seen
                    the drunk driver coming
he would've braced himself. the body's
habitual flexing to make a soft man

harder to snap. in a car crash, it does the opposite.
the same way you can't correct
a steering wheel while spinning out. how we must
loosen ourselves, quickly. sign so many mental treaties

     in exchange for safety.
     both drivers died instantly.

the front-seat passenger wanted to marry my brother.
　　instead, she shattered her pelvis
in twenty-seven places. took her life
when she learned she could no longer
　　carry his child.

i am drawing my brother now, here, in the only way
that is safe for me.
　　he is moving toward me, quickly.
i am flexing.

CALDERA

There is no body to bury. I explain this
to my therapist, ask if a decade is long
enough to declare my brother legally dead—

ask how there can be grief without wisdom
teeth, cracked sternum, caution tape.
Mom says Brian doesn't have a heart

worth hating, says heroin slipped him
quick through the family's tourniquet.
I want to lock my brother in nostalgia's

mausoleum, throw the key in the crematory.
Instead I tuck death in a shoebox
under my bed like a pile of love letters.

My brother is the one who got away,
that good push of hair behind an ear.
I coo his death to sleep, feel its breath

thaw my nipple. When I hear death snore
I yell into the pillow, punch the mattress
until the springs jab back. Into this pot

I toss each spoon my brother burned.
I summon him sober and here.
When he starts to sprint away

I break the line like a femur.

ELEGY FOR THE FOUR CHAMBERS OF MY BROTHER'S HEART

We're under the same moon and I'm sick
    with that knowing. I want to peel it away
like a bumper sticker. Thumbtack Jupiter

    to this storm-angry sky. Jupiter:
Wellbutrin pill tucked behind that dark cloud's
    cauliflower ear. I listen for your name

in all this thunder. Shadows of buildings
    sieve moonlight like a family quilt. The city
empties itself tonight. Lightning stages this

    perfect vacancy like so many camera flashes.
For a moment, you are famous. Even God
    is looking for you.

II

ODE ENDING IN A PHONE CALL

When the lights were on we listened
to albums you stole from a record shop

in Van Nuys. The melody spun liquid,
balsamic black on the turntable.

When the music stopped, Al Green's
"I Can't Get Next to You" was a vesper

for the earthquake dark, early brownouts.
After many mailed threats ripped in two,

Los Angeles really did shut the power off.
It was quiet. We sung low, made shadow

puppets with the tea lights. Our hands twisting
into invented animals, all snout and wing.

When the wicks burned down, we grew tired
of grieving our fingers' extinctions. A decade

dug that needle clean through the vinyl.
Cancer slipped you into that skipping

track's dark orbit. When the first snowstorm
in thirty years killed even your indoor plants

I tried calling, Mom. (I promise.) You're
cutting out (I promise). Are you there?

(I thought I lost you.)

WHAT I HATE MOST ABOUT MOM

is her dying. How these days
I'm busy reckoning

how to make a family
from just one man.

I see death everywhere.
A banana peel left

to the sun is a bat's
cadaver. The accent mark

in every beautiful Spanish
word—la poesía—is a switch

-blade at the belly.
I can look at the knot

in a piece of wood
until it frightens me.

It's November now.
All the leaves are curled

with drought. I lied
before. What I hate

most about my dying
mother is that she

won't eat garlic.
In these final weeks

I try to impress her
with my cooking. She turns

each meal she won't eat
into a rhymed couplet—

When I meet death,
I won't have bad breath.

I'm still learning from her
how to laugh at this poem.

How to turn each bridge
into a balcony. To applaud

everything that floats
downriver. Depending

which way you turn,
the water is coming

or it has already left.

MY BROTHER STOLE EVERY SPOON IN THE HOUSE

so we don't eat soup anymore. We tried. The bone
broth fell right through our forks,

our fingers, stained
the carpets. We all learned to speak twelve languages
but only the words for *good morning*

and *hospital.*
In Old Norse my mom learns the phrase *Where*
are all the fucking spoons? Brian went outside, whispered
swears to the poplars.

They bent their necks to hear him.
Brian went outside

and left forever, took the rest
of the silverware. Brian went outside and left
a thousand doodles he drew,

every happy animal
that wasn't him. We crumpled them like origami

roadkill. Stomped them under our feet until
they became wine between our toes.
We're still drinking it now,

ten years later. I don't know how
magnets work. If I tied a million together, could they
pull him here?

The cutlery turned

ash in his pockets.
Heavy metal in his blood.

ELEGY FOR THE FOUR CHAMBERS OF MY MOTHER'S HEART

You pinch the seam
of a bag of popcorn, swaddle it

like a steaming newborn in the basket
of your walker. Did you know

Orville Redenbacher died sleeping
in a Jacuzzi? *That's how I want to go.*

You're barely making it now
back from the microwave. Your knees,

they tremble like a fresh fawn's.
The beginning of life is too much.

The beginning of life is too much
like the end of it.

SALVATION SONNET

Almost sweetly, the judge gaveled away my summer,
knocking her desk lightly like a quiet neighbor's door.

I worked three hundred hours at a Salvation Army—
their motto *Blood and Fire*. Our small misfit militia,

teenagers unearthing ourselves among the stacks
of orphaned objects, piecemeal Lego sets, doll houses

with missing balconies. Some people would donate
anything for a write-off: prosthetic limbs, uncle's ashes

mistaken for a daisy vase, countless dildos, dildoes, dildi.
I learned the Spanish word—consolador, from *to console*.

We took fishing pictures with the biggest and brightest,
threw them in a box we hid from management

like a pile of armless crosses. Bad cadavers,
sometimes they'd shiver back to life.

MY BROTHER, ASLEEP

Peace lily, arrowhead, aloe.
The last time you went to rehab,

all your houseplants died. Absence parched
the heart of your terra-cotta pots.

Through the keyhole, I watched you eat
your weight in pills. Corkscrew

yourself to sleep in somebody's burnout
pillow fort. On your knees

for those numbing Nordic gods—
Vicodin, Ativan, Tylox. I believed .

you hadn't graduated
to needles again. But you lay

on your side all day. An overdose
can look like the world's

deepest sleep. Once, I saw the secret
rose bed you kept hidden

between your toes. You pushed
perennial seeds into that burned soil.

I put my thumb in your mouth,
slept with you, belly-to-back.

I dreamed that you woke up,
handed me a bouquet.

ELEGY FOR THE FOUR CHAMBERS OF MY HEART

My friend John says the poetry
of earth is never read. So I make a habit
of hiking. I wonder

if my brother ever saw this rock.
If a rock can be sad, then this rock

is sad. It frowns in its strata.
I convince John
to sit on my porch. We set dandelions on fire,
watch them fall

like used matches.

WAITER PARK

The lessons started here: a lowered Honda hatchback that would stall when rolling over even small things. Empty soda cans, the leveled bodies of stray cats, the thick skin of steamrolled basketballs. It was my brother's car. We'd make pit stops at Waiter Park—the nickname Mom gave to the strip of grass where old burnouts waited for their lives to change. Brian would sit in the back seat, window down, trading aluminum foil balls of heroin for wrinkled fives, tens. *You forgot that stop sign back there*, he'd say, taking the wheel from me. Then we'd get cherry slushes mixed with blue raspberry and sit in the car parked outside the gas station. The visor mirror in the passenger seat was missing, but in its place was a sticker that read, *You're Beautiful*. Once, we stalled on a speed bump going home. He tugged that car into neutral, and we both got out to push. I looked at his face, blood-flushed, crack-lipped, scabbed, and shoved my teenage shoulder into the metal. I could feel it. We were beautiful.

AT THE ARCADE I PAINT YOUR FOOTPRINTS

That summer we hopped fences
and called them gates. You'd shark

pool, then we'd hunt deer
with all the quarters you tricked.

You smiled when they leapt
out of view. Passed me

that orange rifle, told me to aim
then close my eyes for ten years.

Antlered brother, Mom
won't sell the house, so you

can have a landmark. Nostalgia rends
in absence. But I remember June—

that last game of foosball,
how we broke off

the little men and shook them
in our hands like tambourines

hoping they'd wake, then run.

REPOSSESSION

To apologize for your vanishing
you brought me a loosie
and a rolled-up *Hustler* and we sat

in your new car trading smoke.
This happened every few months,
our own church service for holiday

Catholics. In that borrowed confessional
you preached what you thought

I'd absolutely need: how to cheat
the cylinder inside a lock,
what words undress
a virgin, how to curse

heaven when things went to hell.
From the passenger seat of that
stolen Cutlass you were a ruined

simile—the way the back
of an empty tow truck looks

like a crucifix. How in the whirling
lights, pressed against that patrol car,

you blushed like a martyr.

LIGHT SHINES THROUGH THE GRISTLE

of a thin cut of bacon's
                              stained glass window—
oh meat, oh meat cathedral. I lost God just once

in a parking lot fight. Jesus's bright-red head

dolloped on His shoulders
like a maraschino cherry. I can't know
                    which punch unwrenched
                    His body

from my silver chain, startling an incisor.
I combed that gravel lot for pocket oxy,
found only orphaned teeth. My brother
tells me the higher the hair,

the closer to God,
                              then pins me down
for buzz cuts.   A priest
on YouTube yells, *Surrender yourself and sing.*

I hold each flat octave in my neck.

I can't lie. There is something

about December. How the carolers in movies
harmonize with suburban doorbells.
                              I feel again
            something like joy,

then watch my brother standing by
our measly Christmas tree, with its

italic lean and aluminum foil star.
            I remember how necessary:
      each ornament, hanging
            from its little noose.

ELEGY FOR THE FOUR CHAMBERS OF MY MOTHER'S HEART

When I was a child you made me hold my breath
driving past cemeteries, under bridges,
through tunnels. We gasped for air

like superstitious carp, tiptoed
around grave plots to honor the dead,
leaped over sidewalk cracks to honor

the living: our mothers, you. You swivel
the bare ball of your foot into each seam
as if it were the cherry of a cigarette.

As if you could design a future for yourself,
trade chemotherapy for a chiropractor.
On that last flight to see you, the pilot joked,

If you insist on smoking, please do it outside.
At the Olive Garden off Sable Boulevard,
you said, *When you're here, your family*

is dying. We push yardsticks of bread down
our trombone throats, wonder how
to prolong a meal that must end.

ELEGY FOR THE FOUR CHAMBERS OF MY BROTHER'S HEART

The sugarcanes we chewed grew in runoff water
from the Tylenol factory. Our daily hunt and gather, first stash
behind Mom's back. We jammed them
between our molars and cheeks
like tobacco, found wild strawberries
big as a boxer's fist. You taught me how to pitch rocks
at the rainwater pond. The slickest stones went farthest,
then sank anyway. That was always the goal, right? To disappear
them into the water, despite our pretending
one might find the other
end.

III

THE GERMAN WORD FOR *HOSPITAL* IS *SICK HOUSE*

and if you die in Amsterdam, a poet
will sing at your funeral. Europeans
got these two things right. At the last apartment

you'll ever live in, I could read Ulysses
before the hot water turns on. A dozen vases
in your cabinets, not a single flower.
    Your death   the last refrigerator

magnet left to collect. You swallow nineteen pills
three times a day. Throw your head back. Your throat,
an hourglass counting. Your body's   drip pan
abacus. I wonder

                how many pounds of you is medicine.

.

The German word for *ambulance*
is *sick car*. The hospital air is hot
sandpaper on my skin. We're here too often.
The nurses call me by my middle name—like I did

something wrong. Your eyes   two ocean buoys
bobbing for air. The body doesn't go easily
but it does go. I daydream the memory
foam pillow I brought you records
    your final, awful yawn.
                    The short life

of a sound. When you die, I'm convinced a bell will ring
in some far place inside me. You said you'd like to run

one day in a field of baby's
breath. In your dreams, all the cellos are near
and out of tune. In my dreams
wind chimes
    spell a word I can't pronounce.

    Your death   the wind. I cannot point to it.
I can point to everything it moves.

LUCKY

The first time I watched *Braveheart*
was in the basement of Lucky's dope house.
I remember the soft cone of light

reaching out from that small box TV
as if asking for spare change from the dark,
how that little glass frame made

blue-faced Wallace look so much
like an action figure (back when Mel
was someone's idea of a hero).

In the downstairs bathroom hung
a cage with Lucky's bird, a gray parrot
he took from a woman who couldn't

pay him. That bird would pull
every dull feather from its back,
curse in Spanish as I watched.

I was nine, alone with *Braveheart*,
that bird, basement boxes I imagined filled
with a life before *Lucky*, when his name

wasn't a character trait. This is how
my brother babysat—upstairs
and horizontal with a needle

sleeping in his bow-tied arm.
Guardian angel taking work naps
among hallway sleeping bags

swollen with strangers
practicing how to be dead.
Lucky's bird downstairs

screaming, *Chinga tu madre.*

ELEGY FOR THE FOUR CHAMBERS OF MY HEART

My dentist is the closest
thing I ever had

to a father. I can't call him
Dad. I call him David.

Our relationship is built
on the fact that I have

cavities and insurance.
On my birthdays, I get form

emails from David's office.
When I reply, *Thanks, Dad,*

I get no response.

ELEGY FOR THE FOUR CHAMBERS OF MY BROTHER'S HEART

To wake me up, you'd press
my tongue to the nipple

of a AA battery. I press
my ear to the door

of AA meetings. Was that
your voice I heard

rejoicing? I'd try anything
to be better than you.

Brother, give me your turmeric
chews, your sexual awakenings,

your coupons for muscle
-building milkshakes, your first

kiss. Give me your vouchers
for one free therapy session.

Shake out your boom box, please.
Press those D-cells to my lips.

H LINE AS METAPHOR

In Denver workdays end standing up
packed like dried fish dry-humping
each other on the H line. Some

passengers, in their drunken wobble
or even in the haze of sobriety,
pull down hard on the rubber handles,

the ones meant for standing,
the ones that swing dumbly above
our heads. They think this action

stops the train. It's all automated,
stopping itself at Broadway,
then Osage, Union Station.

Since the train, as it always does, stops,
the travelers learn to keep tugging.
I can't help but think this is how

prayer works. Like when I prayed
to a god I didn't believe in that your
morphine drip might soothe the wounds

that chemotherapy would not
and how I swear it worked sometimes
but didn't others. Yet in my drunken

sobriety I believe it was me
who eased your pain, my bruised
palms that bleached your blood.

THERE'S A DONUT SHOP IN OJAI, CALIFORNIA

that lets you smoke cigarettes. My brother
exhaled through the fingers of a bear

claw. Our last breakfast together
is caught in my molars. I bite

the memory like a Parliament filter.
He told me the joke about Noah.

How he kept the skunks in a lifeboat
behind the Ark. In that booth

we were sacred just like that, holding
our worst selves behind us—Brian

called himself an angel, held
a glazed ring above his head.

It glistened there, half-eaten.

PORTRAIT OF MY MISSING BROTHER
CAUGHT IN A SPIDERWEB

there's a planet where it rains diamonds

my brother might turn his umbrella
upside down before disappearing

he told me how scared he is
of spiders it's not the legs but all those
eyes he said he never liked being my brother

spent a whole childhood shuffling
cards waiting for the right order we laid
belly down on our living
room floor making history I believe in

his return like I believe in the taste
of bay leaves that the tree outside
my teenage bedroom was a cherry blossom
then one young beloved promised it was
a magnolia while wedding drunk

I heard someone say ornamental pear trees
smell like semen it's your birthday
brother the porch light implodes
the beads of rain caught in the window screen

twilight pearls strangled
by a spiderweb I wait for you
to rematerialize like a coin behind the ear

of my childhood with these eyes
I see you with these eyes

these eyes won't let you leave

WISH

Together, above the kitchen sink, we peeled
a hundred russets. You taught me how
to scoop their eyes out. "If we don't,

they'll watch us eat." The summer
you disappeared I could only fall asleep
in the bathtub. Its porcelain hand cupped
my blueing body. A dozen
candles with their little souls

pinched out. I was angry with want.
I wanted to fold your clothes
while you were still in them. I threw a fistful
of downers into my ogling
mouth. Hoped it'd somehow help me
be my addict brother's brother. It wasn't just
that night but several
years. I courted addiction like I wanted
its last name. I was assembling
a search party inside my body.

A bus driver with swinging crucifix earrings
once told me the rope out of hell

is also on fire. Take these leather gloves
to shield your hands, brother. Know its hide did not save
the bull. Do you remember walking
together? How we'd swing our arms
like dizzy pendulums, keeping
our own time? One night, you accidentally burned

the back of my hand with a cigarette. I see the second
-degree scar—pale scarab bubbling back.
You were apologetic, pulled my hand
toward your face. Pursed your lips and blew

away the ember like a birthday candle. You forgot
to brush away the ash.

LETICIA KNOWS YOUR WEIGHT

The Saturday before junior prom
Tío Cookie died in Flagstaff. Martín joked
you could tell how bad a person is

by how long they wait to masturbate
after a funeral. He said he could
get it up while pallbearing. We were

children then, hanging from
that casket as if from monkey bars.
I learned to wear grief like a wreath

around my neck. Martín's mom, Leticia,
spun us like records under her finger.
She'd guess how much we weighed

within five pounds, yell it proudly
to the block. Her favorite carnival
trick, I'd drop my JanSport and twirl.

She was about our age
when she crossed through El Paso,
worked eighteen-hour days packing

meat, stripping all that silver
skin from piles of beef. Nitrates
tattooing her knuckles.

She told us los muertos son más
pesados que los vivos. She's wrong,
I think—the living are heavier.

We carry the dead on our backs—
they cling to our palms. We hold them up
like shells, moaning in our ears.

ELEGY FOR THE FOUR CHAMBERS OF MY MOTHER'S HEART

In Colorado you work nights
at a call center from your

kitchen table. You swore once
you sold camping gear

to Matthew McConaughey,
kept his credit card number

for a rainy day. The *graveyard
shift* should be illegal, I joke.

You throw your head
back in laughter

like a Disney villain—Ursulaesque.
You say dying doesn't

keep the lights on,
the water heater drooling

in its sarcophagus closet.
But you're off tonight.

You get to sleep in the dark—
like regular people, you say.

LITANY OF BROTHER'S HEIRLOOMS

The fear of birds, but not their music. The small
explosion of gunpowder inside a toy

rocket, but not its parachute down. The ash
limb Tío lathed into a bat. It's always resting

by the front door. The pocket Gideon
and enough spit to cradle a joint

in its thin paper. But not the match
that burned it sermon-quick. The butterfly

knife you found nested in a rain
gutter. The plastic telescope you stole

from a mall kiosk just before my birthday.
The night sky, but not the moon.

WHEN YOU TELL ME YOU'VE GROWN AFRAID

of the dark, it busts every lit bulb
inside me. Please—
put a flashlight in my mouth, Mom.
I will thin
            my cheeks for you.
Let me light the way.

LAKE MENDOTA, AFTER SUNSET

Lake Mendota was previously known as Wonkshekhomikla
("where the man lies") in the original Ho-Chunk

By mid-January this whole lake will freeze over.
A passing stranger tells me this like they had to

get it off their chest. The local hush-hush bubbling
up from the city's slushed lung. At night,

Mendota terrifies me. When the stars un-dim
the Midwest dark is a polishing rag

for its vanity mirror. That trapdoor to some pit
behind my eyes. An idea too far away to see

itself clearly. Under the ice, the fish stop
all their pretending to swim. They're waiting

for the stars to change. Holding their breath for it.
Every day here, the Little Dipper is a little bigger

than me. When I ladle soup into a bowl, I wonder
what the stars name my dipper. If they try to see

themselves in my soup. Maybe I'm too far—
just stubble on Mendota's face. Someone told me

voices carry further over water.
Maybe I terrify them too.

ELEGY FOR THE FOUR CHAMBERS OF MY HEART

I try every day
not to make a metaphor

of every ugly-beautiful thing.

Those two blue birds
blue-birding into dusk
are just jays—not my

reincarnated family.
I blink in Morse code
when passing by strangers,
use jazz hands to let them know

I feel cosmically alone.

Sometimes, from the back
of an empty bus, I gossip
to the driver, tell him

things I don't tell my therapist.
I try every day to make this
poem just a little bit untrue: I grew

four inches this summer.
My immediate family is nearing
extinction. Bob Ross is my uncle.
I don't know how to keep

living anymore. I made
up two of those four facts.
Once, I shot my friend's bow

and arrow straight into
the sun.

IV

ELEGY FOR THE FOUR CHAMBERS OF MY BROTHER'S HEART

You're in a small room cutting
rugs. There's no music playing, no ballad
troubling your movement. Your bony legs
cross each other like witching rods.
When you shimmy the mirrors blush.
You've never looked so alive, down
-lit through the skylight. The stars
are pinholes hemorrhaging moonlight
through a bedsheet. In the dream,
you sashay to the wall of my mind,
waltz through so many handfuls
of silence. You look gorgeous, spinning
the minute hand of a clock—forward
or backward, I can't tell.

DIPTYCH IN A DREAM WHERE THINGS ARE AS THEY SHOULD BE

I.

it's so cold everyone's bundled
like bank robbers ski masks
and balaclavas one man misread
the email as *baklava* and sits
on a park bench rubbing honey
and pine nuts into his beard
phyllo crumbs falling down his parka
and across the street
an every-other-weekend dad
makes pancakes for his son promises
the first one is always the worst
the skillet demands a sacrifice
in the apartment upstairs
a woman tells her beloved
she wants to peel apart
his thighs like two slices
of american cheese his whole
heart a purse dog trembling
he wags his pale ass for that
kraft aphrodite inside the post
office a printer cartridge explodes
they'll have to repaint
the envelopes white again
black ink leaves
ellipses on every
person place or thing

each noun becomes
an omission of words

II.

in the dream things
are as they should be
a dog swallows its own
leash every pawnshop
ring finds a fat finger
a venus flytrap
convinces the room
it's more person than plant
grandma's in the corner
eating poker chips a moth
you nicknamed icarus
sautés against a lightbulb
in the dream your
death is a montage
before a death
the swinging lantern
the flying cinder
smoke plumes billowing
your life collapsing
open like a telescope
I look through
as long as I'm asleep
you aren't dying
is the most
ordinary thing

SELF-PORTRAIT AS MOON CORPSE

Hannah told me happiness is not like riding a bike;
you can forget. It takes eighteen months

                                             to grow an adult
pineapple. Not a single honeyed chunk before then.
It only takes seven months to grow

                     a bastard. If I had a father, he might tell me miracles
take time to root. He'd call me impatient.
I'd call him
              an Uber
to Point Nemo. I was wrong for being

                                        plucked from my unconscious
mother two months early, I know: a blood dam busted

        in her head. She slept for a hundred days,

the adoption papers nearly signed. The rumor goes like this:
                          the same doctor that cradled me

first told her only one of us could live.   Some days I believe that

        is why I'm so fussy with survival. I search for my life

in strangers' wheel wells, under fingernails, halfway up
chimneys, every suburban breakfast nook. The Ouija board said nothing,

        then told me to floss more. The greyhound
        in the neighbor's lawn is wearing a cone of shame.

She looks like a satellite dish hunting the moon. That soundless night-light

we made redundant with our billion bulbs.
That circling corpse shaped after some small planet

uppercut our own.

I want what it has—to be so easily accepted

into someone else's living. Despite whatever happened to us,
we orbit each other.

ELEGY FOR THE FOUR CHAMBERS OF MY HEART

I'm always looking for a mirror
with a family inside it.
If a mirror breaks   which shard
is the family?
         There are so many
ways to hold yourself
hostage. I'm still learning
to love
     my captor.

LATE TO THE SEARCH PARTY

I.

In the Sonoran Desert my brother hands me a revolver. In place of tenderness
he tells me to kill a woodpecker. It's injured, on its back like a sunbather
thrashing in a gravel bed.

My brother stands behind me—

arms around mine like a mini-golf date. Our hands, a nesting
doll with an exploding heart.   A crowd of saguaros

turn their heads to witness.

They multiply in my periphery, hold their hands up
like I'm a cop. I'm crying. I can feel
the trigger even now.   Death's first lesson: I am always

in the present tense. I see the target. My brother's one closed eye
plus mine become a pair

wide open.

On my knees, I make a pit of sun
-hot sand, bury the bird, then the bullet

like the seeds of a flower
        I'm scared will someday grow.

II.

Five years before disappearing, my brother was a florist.

No one believed his hands—knuckles split open
from knife fights, sutured shut at the kitchen table
by our neighbor, the nurse—might grip, peacefully,
a fistful of tulips, hyacinth, baby's breath.

We called his halfway house *church*.
A crucifix above each bed, door, window. Jesus suffered
on every surface. No room for doubt.

The front lawn was patchy as a checkers board. My brother dreamed
of emeralds in a pile of tiger's-eye. He executed

every stage of grief in a Home Depot aisle, saved the money, bought
a sprinkler to cure the disease.
                            Its healing streams like harp strings

slackening in the sun.

III.

The gnats are dozing on my bedroom ceiling. Little silhouettes crouching
in a field of eggshells. In the haze before sleep, I convince myself

they're praying for me

to turn the lamp back on. I'm dimly lit by the alarm clock—

from way up there, I'm the centerpiece

of their modest Sistine Chapel. Hairy-chested god, sprawling
across a wrinkled duvet. In darkness, I hear only their faraway hum, soft
as a vending machine. I dream

of long-stemmed marigolds
                         snaking below
                         a circle of birds.

IV.

In the city of my suffering, I am both dreamer and architect.
I built, for you, a suburb of worship, brother.

The statues I erected look less like you each year,
all smothered in memory's patina.

It's spring now. Here I am, late
to the search party. Uncertain feet

behind my flashlight's beam.
I'm the one to find you.

                    I don't feel grief.

The flashlight aimed at your body

projects a shadow across the mountainside.
      The shadow is the shape
                    of my relief.

ARS POETICA WITH PASSING HAILSTORM

The ceiling is a woman buried upside down.
Let me start again—in Maywood, California, there's a library
that's important to me. Its many ceiling lights: indifferent
glass breasts pointing down at their readers. Each nipple

a gathering of dead moths. At the hospital, I hear
a nurse call cancer *the big casino*
as in *the house always wins*. A house is a many-sided die
always rolling on its spine. I spent
my teenage years watching a good mother lose

her breasts, her hair. She screamed in the shower. She screamed
in the mirror. Each drain wreathed
with death's jet-black wig. There was no *Sesame Street* episode
for this lesson: the first time you see a man's hand

up Cookie Monster's ass, your childhood dies a little. Every day
I wait under passing clouds, feverish and eager
to see a flash of skin. Maybe a wrist, something hairy and flesh-colored
to point my pitchfork at. After that last hailstorm

the front yard looked like a fancy party
where the guests lost all their pearls.
Watch me busy myself with finishing line,
string each bead of ice together. Let me start again—

this is a gift quickly melting in my hands.

ELEGY FOR THE FOUR CHAMBERS OF MY MOTHER'S HEART

This is an elegy, and believe me, it will end
within the small walls of your townhome.

And because I am selfish it ends with your
words and a memory of just you and me

standing above your kitchen sink, pouring
water into an ice cube tray. You tell me

to watch as the water fills up one corner,
then overflows into every empty square.

This, you say, this is how I love you.

NOTES

The poem "When the Body Says No but You Can't Stop Swallowing" borrows its title from the first line of "On Being Suicidal" by b:william bearhart.

The poem "What I Hate Most about Mom" contains a quote often attributed to William Blake.

The poem "My Brother, Asleep" borrows a line from "Elegy for the Saint of Letting Small Fish Go" by Eliot Khalil Wilson.

The poem "Elegy for the Four Chambers of My Heart ['My friend John says the poetry']" contains a misreading of a line from "On the Grasshopper and Cricket" by John Keats.

The phrase "awful yawn," which appears in the poem "The German Word for *Hospital* Is *Sick House*," is inspired by the song "The Awefull Yawn" by Saintseneca.

The poem "Self-Portrait as Moon Corpse" borrows a line from "Learned Happiness" by Hannah Dellabella.

The fourth section of the poem "Late to the Search Party" borrows a line from "The Search Party" by William Matthews.

The poem "Ars Poetica with Passing Hailstorm" contains an image inspired by "X [I found a small ring]" by Matt Rasmussen.

ACKNOWLEDGMENTS

Thank you to the readers, editors, and staff at the following publications for first acknowledging the poems in this manuscript, sometimes published under different names and in different forms:

The Adroit Journal, AGNI, The Boiler, Booth, Colorado Review, Copper Nickel, Cosmonauts Avenue, Cream City Review, Guernica, Gulf Coast, The Journal, Kenyon Review, Muzzle Magazine, New Ohio Review, Ninth Letter, Passages North, The Pinch, Poetry, Poetry Daily, The Rumpus, Salt Hill, Southeast Review, Split Lip Magazine, Variant Lit, VQR, and Waxwing.

"Salvation Sonnet" was reprinted in Best New Poets (2020), edited by Jeb Livingood and Brian Teare. "Elegy for the Four Chambers of My Brother's Heart" was reprinted in Best New Poets (2022), edited by Jeb Livingood and Paula Bohince. "When the Body Says No but You Can't Stop Swallowing" was reprinted in Pushcart Prize XLVII (2023), edited by Bill Henderson. "Wish," previously titled "Search Party," was reprinted in Best of the Net (2024), edited by Tennison Black and Darren C. Demaree. The poem "At the Arcade I Paint Your Footprints" appears in Sarabande's Another Last Call anthology—edited by Kaveh Akbar and Paige Lewis—alongside the poem "My Brother Stole Every Spoon in the House." It also appeared on The Slowdown podcast, then hosted by Ada Limón.

I'd like to thank everyone at Scribner for taking a chance on my debut collection—and especially Kathy Belden, who sits in my corner with a figurative megaphone in hand.

This book would not have been possible without tremendous learning and unlearning by a community of educators, listed here in alphabetical order and with some missing: Kaveh Akbar, Nicky Beer, Marianne Boruch, Roxane Gay, Ilya Kaminsky, Terese Marie Mailhot, Wayne Miller, Beth Nguyen, Don Platt, and Eliot Khalil Wilson.

I am forever indebted to the first readers of this manuscript: Kaveh Akbar, Eloisa Amezcua, Gabrielle Bates, Roxane Gay, K. Iver, Alejandro Lucero, Don Platt, and Jeff Shotts.

I owe a great debt to the poets in my MFA workshops who saw many of these poems in their most vulnerable bodies: Brian, Caleb,

Charlie, Hannah, Jenn, John, Katie, Kelsey, Lucas, Noah, Tamara—and especially Javan, the best guy I ever met.

Thank you to the Ruth Lilly and Dorothy Sargent Rosenberg Fellowship for material support and for introducing me to Bryan Byrdlong, Noor Hindi, Natasha Rao, and Simon Shieh. Their work and care I learn from every day.

Thank you to the Wisconsin Institute for Creative Writing for the time to write and for introducing me to Elijah Bean, Sean Bishop, Yalitza Ferreras, Sadia Hassan, Patrycja Humienik, Nate Marshall, Erika Meitner, Beth Nguyen, Chessy Normile, Amanda Rizkalla, Aurora Shimshak, Taymour Soomro, Alison Thumel, Paul Tran, Mandy Moe Pwint Tu, and Ada Zhang. Their brilliance gives me hope; their friendship gives me life.

Unbudgeable heaps of gratitude to poets Anne Carson, Victoria Chang, Lucille Clifton, Wanda Coleman, Eduardo C. Corral, Mahmoud Darwish, Natalie Diaz, Martín Espada, Ross Gay, Joy Harjo, Terrance Hayes, Fady Joudah, Larry Levis, Federico García Lorca, Shane McCrae, Sjohnna McCray, John Murillo, Diana Khoi Nguyen, Naomi Shihab Nye, José Olivarez, Carl Phillips, Matt Rasmussen, Rainer Maria Rilke, Diane Seuss, Richard Siken, Charles Simic, Danez Smith, Jean Valentine, Vanessa Angélica Villarreal, Jenny Xie, and Ghassan Zaqtan. I stand in the shadow and shade of your words.

Thank you to Los Angeles friends, Aurora friends, Denver friends, Lafayette friends, Austin friends, Madison friends. I am lucky there are too many of you to list.

Thank you to the Madison Arts Commission, mayor Satya Rhodes-Conway, and the alderpeople of Madison for appointing me their seventh poet laureate. Special shout-out to Angie Trudell Vasquez for helping me step into the role with precision and grace.

Thank you, Taylor Kirby, for holding my hand through the voltas.

Thank you, Mom, for my good, thick hair and for teaching me not to be afraid of earthquakes.

Thank you, Brian, for my imagination.

ABOUT THE AUTHOR

Steven Espada Dawson is from East Los Angeles. The son of a Mexican immigrant, he is a former Ruth Lilly Fellow and Wisconsin Institute for Creative Writing Fellow. His poems appear in many journals and have been anthologized in *Best New Poets, Best of the Net, Pushcart Prize,* and Sarabande's *Another Last Call: Poems on Addiction & Deliverance.* He has taught creative writing at universities, libraries, and prisons across the country. He lives in Madison, Wisconsin, where he serves as poet laureate.